The Wonder of Christmas

A Fresh Look at the Story of Christmas

Ron Regenstreif
and
Susan Kunselman

Q4 Impact

17210 Osborne St

Northridge CA 91325

www.myQ4impact.org

ISBN: 979-8-9861649-0-8

Publishing Services provided by BelieversBookServices.com

First Printing: 2022

Printed in The United States of America

Endorsements

"I was so touched as I was reminded about the details of Jesus' birth through the reading of this book! Thank you for taking me to a Holy place of reverence for God's masterful use of the details, and to be humbly obedient no matter the circumstances, and reminding me that our God is with us in the darkness where we bring the light of God's love to the world...!"

Carol Hart, Founder/President,
ZOE International

"*The Wonder of Christmas* is a masterpiece that brings to life the story of Christmas in fresh and enlightening ways. Children, parents, and grand-parents alike will be blessed and inspired in gaining a deeper and meaningful understanding of the Savior's entry into our world. Historical, insightful, and easy to read, *The Wonder of Christmas* should be on every coffee table - drawing families near to Jesus."

Steve Bundy, Senior Vice President, Joni and Friends International Disability Center

Contents

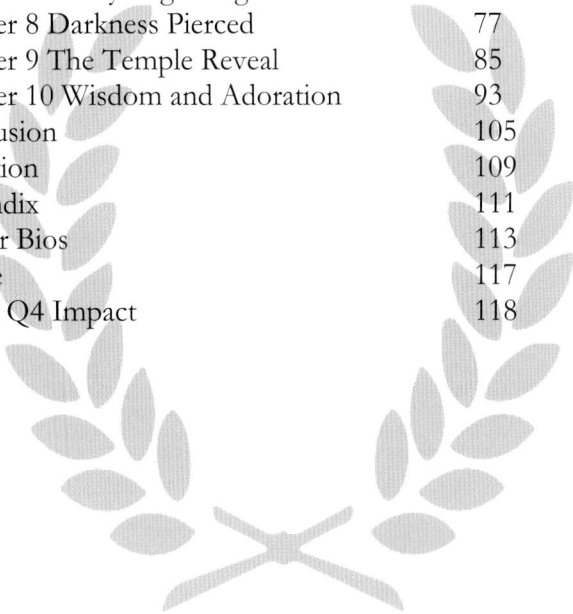

Dedications

To my wife, Roxann, who helped create the
Christmas Eve setting in our home and to my
three sons, their wives, and our eight
grandchildren who have carried on our
family tradition.

I love you all, Poppy (Ron)

To my son, Micah, who reveals God's wonder
and love to me each day. May your heart
always seek the Savior.

I love you, Mom (Susan)

Preface

The personal connection we experience with any story largely stems from being able to enter the world of the characters about whom the story is written. How many times have you read the biblical account of the "Christmas Story," dutifully reading the names and places included in the Gospels while primarily focusing on just the "big events"? What if doing so has limited your *personal* experience with all the stories within THE STORY?

I (Ron) came to know the Lord as my Savior in 1973. The reading of the scriptures brought me to salvation, and I have had a love for God's Word ever since. When my three sons were still young, my passion for giving Jesus a tangible, personal part of our family's Christmas experience became a priority. As I recognized the breadth and depth of the wonders within the story of Christmas, I was motivated to share it. Out of this passion, my wife, Roxann, and I began our tradition of gathering family and friends on Christmas Eve to read the story of Jesus' birth. We began this practice in the early 1980s and, by God's grace, have done so every year since. Rather than becoming repetitive and dull, our love for the Christmas story has grown through the years as God continues to reveal the wonders of His power and purposes in the events of Jesus' birth.

Early in the 2010s, as I became increasingly conscious of how Jesus was taking a backseat to the cultural traditions that are part of most Christmas celebrations, I wondered how this tradition could be replicated among more families and gatherings. It became my passion to present the inspiration of the Christmas story in such a way that others are encouraged to give it the place it rightfully deserves.

As you can see, it has taken many more years to allow for the creation of this book. I hope that this conversational retelling of the Christmas story will make it easy for you to both read and incorporate it into your own Christmas tradition. My prayer is that by highlighting the miracles within the story and offering a broader perspective, you will experience a greater appreciation of God's love and power. May you be freshly inspired by "The Wonder of Christmas!"

I (Susan) met Ron and his family in January 1994. Our friendship grew, and in December of that year, they invited me to their Christmas Eve gathering of friends and family. As expected for a Christmas Eve party, the house was full of laughter, joy-filled conversation, and delicious food! About halfway through the evening, Ron asked everyone to gather in the family room. As an expectant hush fell over the room, Ron announced that his primary delight in hosting such a gathering was to read and remember the reason for our Christmas celebration. After we sang a few carols, Ron began to read the story of Jesus' birth. At times, he would stop and interject his own thoughts about the characters and what they may have been thinking or feeling. He also posed questions to cause us to think more deeply. I came away that night with much more than a full stomach! My heart had been filled with joy and a renewed wonder about the great lengths God took to demonstrate His love for me and for the whole world through the birth of His Son.

While Ron's own excitement over the story of Christ's birth was infectious, he also had an ability to share the Word of God with a focus on God's sovereignty, might, and the wonder of Jesus' birth. Having grown up in a Christian family and accepted Christ at an early age, I had read or heard the Christmas story more times than I could count. Yet, experiencing it in this fresh way ignited a new passion within me. For years, I knew Ron held a desire to create an understandable and con-versational retelling of the Christmas story that would encourage and enable others to incorporate its telling as part of their own Christmas traditions. When he asked if I would help on this project, I jumped at the oppor-tunity to co-write the book you now hold.

This book is for anyone who desires to experience a fresh reawakening to the many miracles and glory pre-sent in the story of Christ's birth. May reading it enable you to know the God of Salvation more deeply through His story.

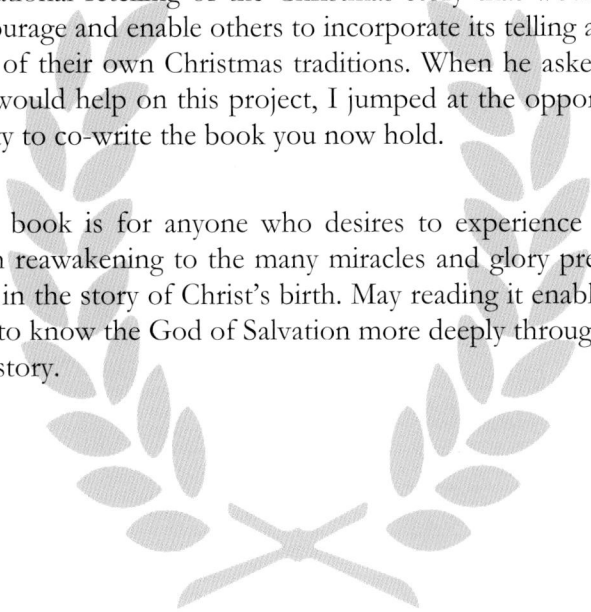

שָׁלוֹם

Introduction

We read in Galatians 4:4: "But when the right time came, God sent his Son…." Have you ever wondered about the details or specifics of "the right time"? For those of us who know God personally, we believe and trust that He is always working out ALL things according to the good purpose of His will for the praise of His Glory (Ephesians 1:11-12, personal translation). Let that sink in: His Sovereignty governs EVERY detail for His purpose! We believe the story of Christmas provides us with many details, which, if excavated well, help us find hidden treasures that will enrich our knowledge and worship of God. Isn't this our goal for the Christmas season, and our entire lives, for that matter?

The Timing of Jesus' Birth

At first glance, "the right time" of Jesus' birth could not have seemed further from right! God's people had not heard from Him for 400 years. His last word had come through the prophet Malachi who predicted that God would send the prophet Elijah before the coming of the Messiah. To say that there was spiritual darkness in the land is an understatement. Even among God's own people, the Israelites, there was constant friction among competing groups regarding how best to practice their faith in God. Politically, the Jewish people lived in an oppressive society. Though no longer slaves in Egypt, they were essentially still exiles in their own country and

heavily taxed by local and faraway rulers. They were ruled by Rome and were subject to the authority of the jealous and paranoid Herod the Great, who had been declared the "King of the Jews" by the Roman senate in 37 B.C. Even Jerusalem, their holy city and the seat of Jewish religious and political practice, would have been considered a police state by today's standards.

It was into this setting that God purposed for Jesus to be born, fulfilling the prophecy in Isaiah 9:2 that "the people who walk in darkness will see a great light. For those who live in a land of deep darkness, a light will shine" (NLT).

Regarding a specific date in history, most scholars place Jesus' birth between 7 B.C. and 4 B.C. If you are like us, this date sounds a bit confusing. For most of our lives,

15

we have heard that B.C. means any date in time BE-FORE the birth of Christ, and A.D. (anno domini, Latin for "in the year of the Lord"), is for any date AFTER Jesus' birth. So how could Jesus have been born "before" he was supposed to have been born?

In the 6th century, when the A.D. system was established, and Jesus' birth was set as A.D. 1, there was very minimal historical knowledge to help them accurately date his birth. The B.C. system did not begin until two centuries later; thus, there was limited understanding of how to count backward. Today, we are fortunate to possess greater knowledge of biblical and historical accounts that inform us of what was occurring in the known world at the time Jesus was born. Though it is still not enough to confirm the exact date of Jesus' birth, the accepted scholarly date of Jesus' birth is good enough for these writers, for it is ultimately our faith in the sovereignty of God over all of history to which we cling (see Hebrews 11:3; Romans 13:1; Ephesians 1:10).

The Original Story Writers and Their Audience

The Gospels of Matthew and Luke provide most of what we consider to be the story of Jesus' birth. Matthew (also referred to as Levi) was one of Jesus' twelve apostles. Though a Jew, Matthew had been a tax collector for Rome before Jesus called him to follow Him. Matthew's account of the birth of Jesus was addressed primarily to the Jews to show that Jesus of Nazareth was the fulfillment of the Old Testament prophesies: he is their Messiah.

On the other hand, Luke was a physician and a close friend and traveling companion of the Apostle Paul. His account of Jesus' birth was taken from other written accounts of the life of Christ and oral reports from eyewitnesses. Because of this, he refers to himself as a historian, backing up the certainty and accuracy of his writing based on his sources and the orderly, thorough account he provides.

The Gospel of Luke and his other book of the Bible—The Book of Acts—are both addressed to Theophilus. While history does not provide much detail or information about Theophilus, Luke's reference to him as "most excellent" (Luke 1:3) indicates he likely held a position of high standing and responsibility in the government. Luke himself was a Gentile, and from the effort he took to explain Jewish customs and substitute Hebrew names with Greek, his book seems more directed toward Gentile readers.

Purpose of this Book

We believe the story of Jesus' birth, as found in the Gospels of Matthew and Luke, is filled with details that, if more clearly grasped, provide an opportunity to connect with the overwhelming GIFT of God's Son more deeply. Just as a child is filled with wonder and delight as they open the gifts under a Christmas tree, our purpose in creating this book is to create fresh wonder and awe as the story of Christmas is shared. We hope this compila-

tion that includes unfamiliar details of the who, what, when, where, and why will serve to reawaken and captivate you with the glory and wonder of the story of Christmas.

Our prayer is that this book draws you toward the story of Christ's birth and that you would become like Mary, who treasured "up all these things in her heart" (Luke 2:19). May such treasuring result in your own glorifying and praise to God during the Christmas season. May you see anew how, as the German architect Mies Van der Rohe points out, "God is in the details" of His story AND yours.

A voice of one crying out: Prepare the way of the Lord in the wilderness; make a straight highway for our God in the desert.

Isaiah 40:3

Chapter 1

The Wonder Begins

The Christmas story begins with an elderly Jewish couple: Zacharias and Elizabeth. Their high standing in the community is revealed through the telling of their ancestry; they are descendants of Aaron, the brother of Moses. In a culture where a family tree carried a great deal of significance, their identity with Aaron resulted in their being viewed as godly people. In addition, the Bible states that they were both righteous in God's sight due to faithfully following all the Lord's commandments and regulations. In the Jewish culture of that era, having children was the evidence of right living. Yet, in Zacharias and Elizabeth's case, no child had been born. They had

undoubtedly prayed for a child for many years and endured the disgrace of being childless, and now they were, by human expectations, much too old to have children naturally.

Zacharias worked as a priest to represent the Jewish people before God, and twice a year, he would go to the temple in Jerusalem to do so. For generations, the Jewish people viewed the inner courts of the temple as the physical location where God Himself was present. This area was comprised of two separate areas known as the Holy Place and Holy of Holies, and ordinary men were not allowed in either of them.

During his time of service at the temple, Zacharias was chosen to enter the Holy Place. It's important to note that Zacharias being chosen was not simply another man's decision. Scripture tells us that he was chosen by lot; thought to be marked stones, lots were widely used by the Jews to ascertain God's will. Zacharias had been selected for the most important job—sprinkling incense on the hot coals and praying for the people of Israel as the smoke rose. "So what?" you may be thinking. But the "what" is actually a "WHO"! The work of the priest points all humanity to Jesus, who would become a sacrifice for all our sins and forever live to pray for us (Ephesians 5:2, Hebrews 7:25).

In this setting, Gabriel, an angel, appears to Zacharias. And though Zacharias had entered the Holy Place, fully expecting God's presence, he was terrified and overwhelmed with fear when the angel of the Lord appeared. The angel's first words to Zacharias, "Don't be afraid!" beautifully illustrate God's care for our human emotions.

The angel went on to say,

> "God has heard your prayer. Your wife, Eliza-
> beth, will give you a son, and you are to name
> him John. You will have great joy and gladness,
> and many will rejoice at his birth, for he will be
> great in the eyes of the Lord. He must never
> touch wine or other alcoholic drinks. He will be
> filled with the Holy Spirit, even before his birth.
> And he will turn many Israelites to the Lord their
> God. He will be a man with the spirit and power
> of Elijah. He will prepare the people for the
> coming of the Lord. He will turn the hearts of
> the fathers to their children, and he will cause
> those who are rebellious to accept the wisdom of
> the godly."

(Luke 1:13-17, NLT)

Have you ever asked God for something repeatedly,
with no answer coming within the timeframe you wanted or felt was right? Zacharias, whose name meant "the
Lord remembers," surely felt the angst of believing his
prayers were either being unanswered or, worse, un-
heard. Yet the appearance of an angel didn't overcome
his doubt that God would fulfill the promise he had just
heard. Seeing only the limitation of his old age, Zacharias asked Gabriel how he could be sure it would happen?
That question turned out to be his last for many months,
as his unwillingness to believe by faith, what the angel
had spoken, resulted in God causing him to be unable to
speak until after John was born.

The simple but meaningful practices of offering a sacri-

fice and praying for the people of Israel took much longer than expected, and those waiting outside became very curious about what was happening. When Zacharias finally exited the temple, the wondering crowd grew confused by Zacharias' inability to speak and his gestures attempting to explain what had happened. He then completed his time of ministering and went home to his wife, Elizabeth.

Not long after, Elizabeth did become pregnant, as the angel had spoken, and for five months, she isolated herself, saying, "How kind the Lord is! He has taken away my disgrace of having no children" (Luke 1:25, NLT).

For a child is born
for us, a son will be
given us, and the
government will be
upon his shoulders.
He will be named
Wonderful
Counselor,
Mighty God,
Eternal Father,
Prince of Peace.
Isaiah 9:6

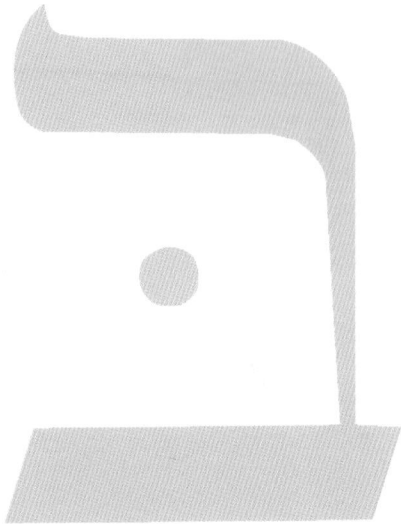

Chapter 2

And You Will Name Him Jesus

As the miracle child grew in Elizabeth's womb, God again sent the angel Gabriel to the village of Nazareth, in the district of Galilee. His purpose? To make the most important birth announcement the world has ever known. Nazareth was a small, secluded village with only about 400-500 people. Surrounded by hills, the landscape of Nazareth was flat, which contributed to its success as a farming community. Part of Roman territory, its population was a mix of Jews and Gentiles. Here, Gabriel appeared to Mary, a virgin, who was engaged to Joseph, a descendant of King David.

In a town with a reputation for poor morals and religious practice, Gabriel's first words stand out: "Greetings, you who are highly favored! The Lord is with you" (Luke 1:28, NIV). What a wonderful reminder of two things. First, Mary lived a life pleasing to God amidst a society not known to reflect the ways of God; and so, for us, as followers of God today, it is likewise possible to live for God in our current society (see John 15:19). Second, just as God saw and knew Mary intimately—her heart, circumstances, hopes, and dreams, we can also find joy in being truly seen and known by God Himself (see Psalm 139:1-3; Genesis 16:13).

Similar to Zacharias' response to Gabriel's greeting, we are told that when the angel appeared, Mary was "deeply troubled" and wondered what was to come. Gabriel's message continued,

> "Do not be afraid, Mary, for you have found favor with God. Now listen: You will conceive and give birth to a son, and you will name him Jesus. He will be great and will be called the Son of the Most High, and the Lord God will give him the throne of his father David. He will reign over the house of Jacob forever, and his kingdom will have no end."

(Luke 1:30-33)

Again, like Zacharias, Mary asked the angel a question in response to the humanly impossible pronouncement that had just been made. Yet Gabriel's very different reply to Mary should make us question, Why the difference? Scripture says Mary asked the angel, "How can this be, since I have not had sexual relations with a man?" (Luke 1:34).

If you recall from the previous chapter, the essence of Zacharias' question was, "How can I know this?" Though seemingly similar at first, the motivation underlying each question varied greatly. Zacharias wanted assurance and certainty, thus reflecting his doubt and unbelief. Mary's question reflected her faithful acceptance while wondering how God would accomplish this miracle. As the whole of scripture teaches us, God knows our hearts and minds (I Samuel 16:7), so it is reasonable to state that the different outcome to their questions was due to the condition of their hearts.

In response to Mary's curiosity, Gabriel explained, "The Holy Spirit will come upon you, and the power of the Most High will overshadow you. Therefore, the holy one to be born will be called the Son of God" (Luke 1:35). He went on to tell Mary that her relative, Elizabeth, had also conceived a child, despite being too old, and was in her sixth month of pregnancy.

Just as the angel's words had begun with sensitivity to Mary's fear, he ended his message with encouragement to Mary's faith, stating, "For nothing will be impossible with God" (v. 37). In humble response, Mary replied, "I am the Lord's servant. May it happen to me as you have said." (v. 38, author's paraphrase).

Then the angel departed.

My soul
magnifies the Lord,
and my spirit
rejoices in God
my Savior.
Luke 1:46–47

Chapter 3

What A Greeting!

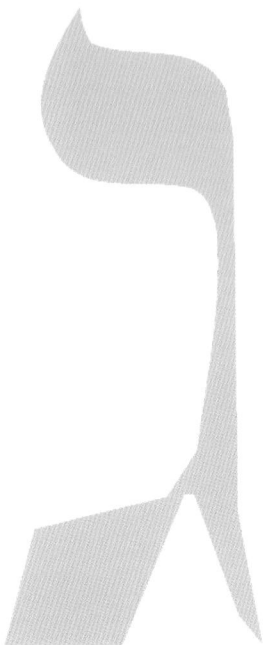

In Luke, we are told that after the angel left her, Mary "set out and hurried to a town in the hill country of Judah" (1:39) to visit Elizabeth. Though it is not precisely known how they were related, we know that despite their significant age difference, they were relatives who loved one another and now had much in common. They had both found favor with God and would give birth to children to fulfill prophecies. [1]

There were likely numerous reasons Mary chose to travel from Nazareth to the home of Zacharias and Elizabeth. Perhaps fear gripped her as she anticipated the gossip and ridicule and the resulting loss of reputation once it was known she was pregnant without being mar-

1. See the appendix for a list of the primary prophecies fulfilled in Jesus' birth

ried. She knew that Elizabeth had faithfully endured much of the same during the many years she was childless and, as a result, would offer her empathy and protection. Another motivation may have been her desire to rejoice with her relative over the child that had been promised. And what young, pregnant girl in those circumstances does not need encouragement! Whatever her reasons, they were compelling enough to overcome the challenging travel it required for Mary. The distance between their homes was approximately 100 miles, involving a dirt path through a mountainous region and over 1,000 feet of uphill hiking. Mary would have likely traveled with a group to give protection against robbers that lurked along the path, and the trip would have taken five to six days.

Upon arriving at her destination, Mary entered the home of Zacharias and Elizabeth. We can all relate to the excitement of hearing a loving voice in an unexpected greeting. Luke tells us that when Elizabeth heard Mary's greeting, her excitement included the baby jumping within her and the Holy Spirit giving her these words: "Blessed are you among women, and your child will be blessed! How could this happen to me, that the mother of my Lord should come to me? For you see, when the sound of your greeting reached my ears, the baby leaped for joy inside of me. Blessed is she who has believed that the Lord would fulfill what he has spoken to her!" (Luke 1:42-45).

At this point, Mary could have been only a few weeks pregnant. The Son of God—Jesus—developing in her womb would not have been evident, nor had Mary had the opportunity to share a single detail or reason for her visit. Yet as Elizabeth's words reflect, the Holy Spirit caused her and her baby to worship. What a greeting!

Can you imagine what Elizabeth's words would have meant to a young girl who was perhaps wrestling with both faith and fear and possibly experiencing a bit of morning sickness? Calling her blessed, affirming her faith, and acknowledging that her baby would be Lord and Savior would have been a confirmation to Mary of all the angel, Gabriel, had spoken to her. What was Mary's response to Elizabeth's greeting? She also worshipped! In the portion of scripture that has been titled *The Magnificat* (meaning "it magnifies"), Mary said,

My soul magnifies the Lord,
and my spirit rejoices in God my Savior,
because he has looked with favor
on the humble condition of his servant.
Surely, from now on all generations
will call me blessed,
because the Mighty One
has done great things for me,
and his name is holy.
His mercy is from generation to generation
on those who fear him.
He has done a mighty deed with his arm;
he has scattered the proud
because of the thoughts of their hearts;
he has toppled the mighty from their thrones
and exalted the lowly.
He has satisfied the hungry with good things
and sent the rich away empty.
He has helped his servant Israel,
remembering his mercy
to Abraham and his descendants forever,
just as he spoke to our ancestors.
(Luke 1:46-55)

Mary's praise to God revealed how much she knew of the (Old Testament) scriptures and their prophecies about the Messiah. Though she would have only heard the reading of the scriptures in her local synagogue, she not only retained the words but also understood much of what they meant about the baby she now carried. Her praise reflected passages from numerous scriptures, re-

vealing her awareness of her Son's future miracles and the judgment and salvation He would bring.

Mary would have been like any woman who, upon learning they are pregnant, are filled with wonder and hope for what their child will be. Today, many mothers-to-be are blessed by medical technology that enables them to learn much about their child before birth. In Mary's case, it wasn't an ultrasound that gave her insight into her child but the "soundness" of the Hebrew scriptures.

We are told that Mary stayed with Zacharias and Elizabeth for three months before returning home. You may recall that Zacharias was a priest and, as such, would have had both in-depth knowledge and access to the scriptures. Could it be that much of their time together was spent studying those scriptures? What an encouragement they must have been to one another! Their time together also provides a beautiful picture of God's care for the details: He orchestrated the support and encouragement of His children through His Word and one another.

See, I am going to
send my messenger,
and he will clear
the way before me.
Malachi 3:1

Chapter 4

His Name Is John

The first chapter of Luke ends with the fulfillment of the first birth announcement made by the angel, Gabriel—Elizabeth gave birth to a son. It was humanly impossible for Elizabeth to have a child, yet God's promise had been fulfilled! Everyone loves a good story, and this one spread like wildfire! Gabriel had proclaimed to Zacharias that "many will rejoice with you," and Luke 1:58 tells us that, indeed, their neighbors and relatives rejoiced with Elizabeth over the incredible kindness and mercy of the Lord.

46

When the baby was eight days old, all their relatives and friends came for the circumcision ceremony. This ceremony, today referred to as a *bris*, was of enormous significance in the lives of Jewish families. God initiated the practice of circumcision for Jewish males. It served as an external sign of His covenant, or commitment, to His chosen people. First begun with Abraham, known as the father of the Jewish people, circumcision was to be a symbol of a life set apart for God (Genesis 17:10-14). Though Zacharias and Elizabeth's son was born over 1,700 years after Abraham, they faithfully followed this tradition. Such a ceremony included the speaking of blessings over the child and the formal announcement of the child's name.

Everyone who attended Zacharias' and Elizabeth's ceremony assumed that, in keeping with tradition, the baby would be named Zacharias (after his father). But when the time came to announce his name, Elizabeth said, "No! He must be named John." Those around her were shocked, and confusion set in. In response, Zacharias used a writing tablet and wrote, "His name is John!"(Luke 1:63, NLT). Instantly, Zacharias could speak again, and he began praising God!

At this time, Zacharias was also filled with the Holy Spirit and said,

> "Blessed is the Lord, the God of Israel, because he has visited and provided redemption for his people. He has raised up a horn of salvation for us in the house of his servant David, just as he spoke by the mouth of his holy prophets in ancient times; salvation from our enemies and from the hand of those who hate us. He has dealt mercifully with our fathers and remembered his holy covenant – the oath that he swore to our father Abraham. He has given us the privilege, since we have been rescued from the hand of our enemies, to serve him without fear in holiness and righteousness in his presence all our days. And you, child, will be called a prophet of the Most High, for you will go before the Lord to prepare his ways, to give his people knowledge of salvation through the forgiveness of their sins. Because of our God's merciful compassion, the dawn from on high will visit us to shine on those who live in darkness and the shadow of death, to guide our feet into the way of peace." (Luke 1:68-79)

All their neighbors were astonished and filled with reverence for God. Just as big news travels quickly today, the miraculous news of John's birth, naming, and the prophetic word about him spread throughout the surrounding hill country of Judea. This hill country, also known as the Judean or Hebron Mountains, included the cities of Jerusalem and Bethlehem.

We are told that everyone who heard the news contemplated it deeply and wondered what John would turn out to be, for they recognized that the Lord was with him. Talk about "being set apart for God"! Just think, even before John was two weeks old, news of him spread to the very locations that would soon hear his teaching on the need for repentance and baptism as he proclaimed the coming Messiah.

Please don't miss that while John was chosen to prepare the way for the Lord, God also prepared John's way. What a beautiful reminder of the same promise we have for our lives today; Psalm 48:14 states, "This God is our God for ever and ever. He will be our guide even to the end" (NIV).

We know from scripture that John grew up, became strong in spirit, and remained in the wilderness. It was there that God's word came to him, and his ministry began. The gospels of both Luke and Mark declare that John and his ministry fulfilled what the prophet, Isaiah, had written: "See, I am sending my messenger ahead of you; he will prepare your way. A voice of one crying out in the wilderness: Prepare the way for the Lord; make his paths straight!" (Mark 1:2-3).

God's great rescue plan for
His people had begun!

Obedience to Christ doesn't mean following Him to some destination. A life of obedience never really comes in for a landing.

Ellen Vaughn—
author
On Becoming
Elisabeth Elliott

Chapter 5

Fathering the Savior

So far in our story, we have seen how God chose Zacharias and Elizabeth to be John's parents. We saw how he chose and filled John with the Holy Spirit, even before he was born (Luke 1:15), and called him the one who would announce the coming of Jesus. We've also learned that God chose Mary to conceive and give birth to the Son of God miraculously. But what of an earthly father for God's Son? How would God accomplish this?

Yes, Mary was engaged to a man named Joseph, but now that she was already pregnant before their marriage, he would likely believe Mary had been unfaithful. As she returned home from her visit with Elizabeth, now visibly pregnant, Mary knew that she would face disgrace and hurtful gossip. Mary and Joseph lived at a time when an engagement was viewed much more seriously than it is today. The only way it could be broken was through a divorce. Couples did not live together during the engagement period, and pregnancy before marriage would have been treated as adultery and could even have been punished by death.

It's likely Mary shared with Joseph all the angel, Gabriel, had spoken to her and recounted to him the miraculous conception and birth of John. But could Joseph believe her story when no pregnancy in human history had ever occurred outside of the natural way? In addition, Joseph would have also faced his own dishonor, as it would have been assumed by others that Joseph was Mary's partner in adultery. Yet we are told in Matthew 1:19 that Joseph was a righteous man. As such, he didn't act hastily or out of anger to protect his reputation. Joseph loved Mary and desired to show mercy, but how could he believe such an impossible story was true? As he wrestled with the decision before him, he decided to divorce her secretly, hoping she would not face more public humiliation.

It was at this point that God stepped in. Joseph had made a kind decision but had not yet acted on it. Then, an angel of the Lord appeared to him in a dream, saying, "Joseph, son of David, don't be afraid to take Mary as your wife, because what has been conceived in her is from the Holy Spirit. She will give birth to a son, and you are to name him Jesus, because he will save his people from their sins" (Matthew 1:20).

The Gospel of Matthew states that the angel's words to Joseph fulfilled what the Lord had spoken through the prophet Isaiah at least 700 years prior, "See the virgin will become pregnant and give birth to a son, and they will name him Immanuel" (1:23; see also Isaiah 7:14).

Don't you just love how specific God is? Every single word He speaks is intentional and purposeful. Isaiah 55:11 says, "so is my word that goes out from my mouth; It will not return to me empty, but will accomplish what I desire and achieve the purpose for which I sent it."

When the angel addressed Joseph as "son of David," those words would have reminded him of his royal family line and prepared him for the coming of his long-awaited Messiah-King. The message then provided peace for Joseph's turbulent emotions, confirmed the truth of how Mary's child was conceived, and gave very clear direction on what he was to do. Indeed, the Lord's message to Joseph in his dream accomplished ALL for which it was sent. We are told in Matthew 1:24 that "when Joseph woke up, he did as the Lord's angel had commanded him."

Do you think doing what the angel commanded suddenly became easy for Joseph? Yes, the Bible describes Joseph as a "righteous man," and he was also still very human. Yet, despite nagging doubts and questions that remained unanswered, he chose to obey the word of God, even at personal cost.

While the Gospels reveal a few more details about Joseph—the earthly father of Jesus, we know very little about him. Could it be that even the Bible's lack of words about Joseph speaks much? We don't know his age, anything about his family and friends, or his thoughts and emotions about the role to which God called him. In the absence of such details, what does stand out is that God chose to use an ordinary man who was willing to obey Him by faith through difficulties and without fame. The apostle Paul reiterates this in I Corinthians 1:26-27, stating that God does not choose His followers based on their wisdom, influence, or position in life. Rather, like Joseph, we are each called "to the obedience that comes from faith" (Romans 1:5, NIV). Just as Joseph's faithful obedience allowed him the privilege of being a firsthand witness of God coming into the world in human form, imagine how God may choose to use your faithful obedience as a witness to your world of who Jesus Christ is and all He has done!

Bethlehem Ephrathah, you are small among the clans of Judah; one will come from you to be ruler over Israel for me.

Micah 5:2

Chapter 6

Return to Bethlehem

In the introduction, we learned that the Jewish people lived under Roman rule at the time of Jesus' birth. As a people that Rome had conquered, they were allowed to maintain their spiritual beliefs and customs, but otherwise, they did what they were told. Thus, when the Roman government decreed a census to count the people to assess taxes, they had to comply.

Luke 2 explains that the census required everyone to go to their hometown. Roman history also supports this detail, for their practice was to count by households so that people and property would be taxed by families. Thus, "Joseph also went up from the town of Nazareth in Galilee to Judea, to the city of David, which is called Bethlehem, because he was of the house and family line of David, to be registered along with Mary, who was engaged to him and was pregnant" (Luke 2:4-5).

For most pregnant women close to their time of giving birth, a tiring road trip is generally not desired. Mary, who was in the uncomfortable stage of pregnancy, would have been no different. Yet could she and Joseph have found strength and encouragement as they considered how God was orchestrating the details for the birth of His Son? We already learned that Mary and Joseph were familiar with the scriptures and the prophecies regarding Israel's Messiah. Perhaps they recalled the words of Micah 5:2, which declared that the Messiah would come out of Bethlehem. Yes, the census required them to leave Nazareth, but could they have recognized God's Sovereign hand using the inconvenient and stressful journey to accomplish His promises?

However, recognizing God at work would not have changed the difficulty of their trip to Bethlehem. Mary and Joseph would have had to travel eighty to ninety miles depending on their route. Their journey would have taken a week to ten days through flat, desert valleys and across rocky hills. We have all seen pictures of Mary riding on a donkey, yet scripture does not make this clear. In fact, given the stubborn nature of donkeys and the discomfort of riding on one (even when not pregnant), it is more likely that Mary walked most of the way.

Many translations of the Bible state that upon arriving in Bethlehem, "there was no room for them in the inn" (Luke 2:7, NIV). While there were inns during this time (like we think of hotels today), the Greek word used by the author of Luke is best translated as "guest room." Remember that since Joseph's family came from Bethlehem, it would have been likely that he had relatives there with whom they hoped to stay. Whether they sought a guest room at a relative's home or public ac-

commodation, none were available to them because of all the people also there for the census.

Our story shows that the unfolding of God's plans and the fulfillment of His promises do not equate to an easy path for those who follow Him. Yet despite ongoing hardship, Mary and Joseph exhibit faithful, humble obedience to God. They knew the One who had called them and chose to trust His Words. We have the same choice. Will we also trust Him even amid the most difficult of circumstances?

He came unto his
own, and his own
received him not.

John 1:11

KJV

Chapter 7

Lowly Beginning

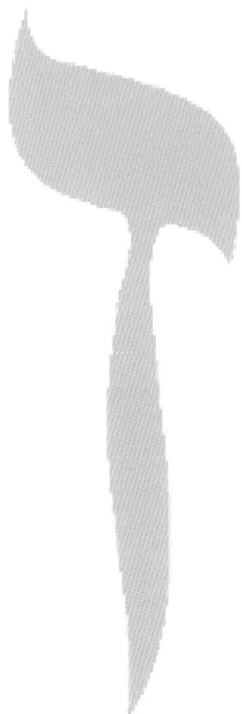

The Son of God was about to enter the world He had made, and not a single guest room was available. The God of all creation could have easily arranged a fitting space for the entrance of the King of Glory—a place of comfort and ease for Mary and Joseph. Yet His perfect plan included the humblest of entries and required Mary and Joseph's continued, humble acceptance of God's plan.

In the Old Testament, God revealed His presence to Elijah in a gentle whisper (I Kings 19:11-12). In like manner, the presence of the incarnate God in the form

of a baby came quietly and without fanfare: "While they were there, the time came for her to give birth. Then she gave birth to her firstborn son, and she wrapped him tightly in cloth and laid him in a manger, because there was no guest room available for them" (Luke 2:6-7).

Can you imagine it? You've just spent the last week or more traveling over rugged terrain and have arrived at your destination exhausted and dirty. You hold the hope of lodging because you have family in this town, or at the very least, you anticipate the kindness of being offered a guest room. Instead, the only welcome received is "no vacancy."

A natural response to such treatment could easily have been frustration and impatience, fueled by exhaustion and anxiety over the thought of giving birth with no shelter or privacy. Yet as past behavior is often the most accurate predictor of future behavior, it is more probable that Mary and Joseph had a supernatural response; their reaction likely reflected their humility in submitting to God's plans and trusting His care.

In his fictional work *Mary*, Sholem Asch ascribes these words to Mary upon finding shelter in a stable, "Perhaps it is God's will that my child see the light of the world among the humble and poor." Have you ever seriously considered the heart and mind of God demonstrated in this detail? He is the Creator of the world and everything in it, the God who gives life and breath to all and who does not live in man-made structures. Before the world's creation, God planned to send His Son, Jesus, the one before whom every knee will one day bow. The

one who humbly gave up His position in heaven so that we might see the glory of God.

Jesus knew we could never do or be enough in our own strength to bridge the gap between a sinful man and a holy God. This truth was evidenced by how burdensome the Jewish worship of God had become at that time in history. The prevailing teaching presented by the Jewish rabbis declared that only those considered "ceremonially clean" were worthy to enter the synagogues—let alone be accepted by a holy God. It was into that separation between God and man that "God so loved the world" (John 3:16, NIV) that HE chose to come close to us. And He did it without showiness or applause, causing His only and much-loved Son to come in the form of a baby born in a messy stable.

In the first chapter of the Gospel of John, we are told that the One who created the world and set the lights in the heavens, who is Himself the Light, came into the world to give light to everyone. Jesus came into the darkness and messiness of the world at that time, and His light STILL comes into the darkness and messiness of our world and lives today. This is the Good News: the darkness did not and cannot overcome His light!

Jesus entered the world that first Christmas morning in the lowliest of places and with the gentleness of a baby. Later, during His ministry, Jesus described His own heart as gentle and lowly toward all who are weary and burdened (Matthew 11:29). Will you let the example of Mary, Joseph, and the baby, Jesus, serve as a reminder that God still desires to come close in your darkness and messiness? Will you choose to follow the example of

Mary and Joseph, who were willing to obey and remain humbly obedient despite unmet expectations and hardship?

Jesus came for one reason: to offer Himself as the perfect sacrifice for our sins through His death on a cross, so that all who believe in Him as their Savior might be restored to relationship with God. In the fulfillment of prophecy, a child HAS been born; a Son HAS been given. He is the risen King of Kings. May you experience Him this Christmas as your "Wonderful Counselor, Mighty God, Everlasting Father, Prince of Peace" (Isaiah 9:6, NLT).

The people who
live in darkness
have seen a great
light, and for those
living in the land
of the shadow of
death, a light has
dawned.

Matthew 4:16

Chapter 8

Darkness Pierced

In Luke 2:8, we are told that when Jesus was born, shepherds were staying out in the fields watching over their flock of sheep at night. The city of Bethlehem, where Jesus was born, was only five and a half miles from the Jewish capital of Jerusalem. In the fields surrounding the city, lambs were born and raised—lambs pure enough to be used for the Passover sacrifices. The shepherds of these special sheep worked at an occupation passed down to them for generations. Like all shepherds, they were trained to care for these sheep, even at the risk of their own lives.

Since the shepherd's primary job was to protect the sheep, they likely had a heightened sense of alertness at night to guard against predators. Yet nothing could have prepared them when "… an angel of the Lord stood before them, and the glory of the Lord shone around them" (Luke 2:9). Do you think you would be startled and scared by such an appearance? Luke goes on to tell us that "they were terrified!" Think of it. Only starlight and perhaps a few fires dispersed the thick darkness of the night, yet when The Light of the world was born, His glory itself shone in the fields and pierced the darkness with heavenly light!

Consistent with the same message spoken by the angels who appeared in person to Zacharias and Mary and to Joseph in a dream, the angel said to the shepherds, "Don't be afraid!" Continuing, he said, "I proclaim to you good news of great joy that will be for all people. Today in the city of David a Savior was born for you, who is the Messiah, the Lord. This will be a sign for you: You will find a baby wrapped tightly in cloth and lying in a manger." (Luke 2:10-12).

Just as the sheep in the fields around Bethlehem were special sheep, so these shepherds were much more than ordinary shepherds. Known as Levitical shepherds, they would have been familiar with Hebrew writings and the Law of Moses. Thus, they would have known the prophecies of the long-awaited Messiah and the significance of the angel's pronouncement of the baby being wrapped in cloth and lying in a manger, for only perfect lambs were treated this way to signify that they would be an acceptable sacrifice. In short, the angel had just announced that baby Jesus was the Lamb of God who would take away the sin of the world through His own sacrificial death! What's more, the angel's statement that Jesus' birth was good news for ALL people reinforced God's promise to Abraham that he would be the father of many nations (Genesis 17:5). Several decades would pass before the Good News of Jesus as the Savior for ALL people would be preached among those who were not Jewish. Yet God's plan to conquer sin and make peace between Himself and man had begun.

As the shepherds we e likely still trying to process the reality and significar e of what the angel had told them,

"Suddenly there was a multitude of the heavenly host with the angel, praising God and saying: Glory to God in the highest heaven, and peace on earth to people he favors!" (Luke 2:13-14).

Then the angels returned to heaven as quickly as they had appeared, and immediately, the shepherds went into Bethlehem to see with their own eyes what had been made known to them. Luke 2:16 tells us they "…found both Mary and Joseph, and the baby who was lying in the manger."

Luke tells us that after this, the shepherds returned to their fields. But don't think for a moment that their story ended there! Amidst giving praise and glory to God, they also shared with everyone the message they had witnessed and heard. Yes, they knew what it was to shepherd sheep, and that night, they understood a baby had been born who would be "a ruler who will shepherd my people Israel." (Matthew 2:6).

For there is nothing hidden that will not be revealed, and nothing concealed that will not be brought to light.

Mark 4:22

Chapter 9

The Temple Reveal

You may have heard it said that with God, there are no coincidences. Time and again, this story has revealed how God is in control over every single detail. This chapter will explore what occurred in the first forty days of Jesus' life and the amazing significance these often-overlooked events hold.

Think back with us about some of the key individuals God hand-picked to play a role in Jesus' birth. Do you

remember how they are described? Zacharias and Elizabeth were called "righteous in God's sight." Mary was
"favored." And Joseph was "a righteous man." Yet we
are told in both the Old and New Testaments that there
is no one righteous—that is, sinless—on the earth
(Ecclesiastes 7:20). So, what did their righteousness
mean?

While scriptures reveal that an aspect of being called righteous had to do with obeying God's commands and requirements, we know from I Samuel 16:7 that the Lord sees and desires a person's heart over their appearance or behaviors. Psalm 40:8, which says, "I desire to do your will, O my God; your law is within my heart," gives us a clue to the kind of righteousness that existed in those God chose to play a part in Jesus' birth. Even God's revelation of Himself and His plans to them did not 'give license' or cause them to disregard the religious commands and requirements of their day. Rather, their lives revealed a sincere desire to obey and please God, for they understood that in their fulfillment, God's intent was that they would see and experience Him.

Thus, when Jesus was born, Mary and Joseph followed the requirements given to Moses (Leviticus 12:1-4, 6-8) for Jesus' dedication to God and Mary's purification. From Luke 2:21-24, we see that Mary and Joseph circumcised Jesus on the eighth day of his life and that thirty-three days later, they went to Jerusalem to dedicate him to God with a sacrifice.

While they were in the temple in Jerusalem, we learn of Simeon, yet another man described as "righteous and devout." Luke 2:25-26 tells us that Simeon was "looking forward to Israel's consolation, and the Holy Spirit was on him." He had also received with faith his message from the Holy Spirit: he would not die before he saw the Lord's Messiah. It was no coincidence that on the very day Mary and Joseph went to dedicate Jesus at the temple, Simeon was also there, guided by the Holy Spirit.

Scripture does not tell us *how* he knew, but we are told that when Simeon saw Jesus, he took him up in his arms and praised God! In what has become known as the *Nunc Dimittis*, Latin for the *Song of Simeon*, Simeon praised God for fulfilling His promise to him and declared to all present that Jesus was the Messiah. Having listened to and obeyed God with his whole heart, God blessed Simeon with eyes to see that this child, though not yet even two months old, was the long-awaited Hope of salvation for Israel and all people. God also caused Simeon to prophesy of Jesus' life, ministry, and death, revealing that each person's response to Jesus would determine their own future.

As if Simeon's prophetic words were not enough to

bring speechless amazement to his hearers, at the very moment he stopped speaking, another took up the cry! Anna, a widow of eighty-four years and a prophetess, had served God at the temple night and day with fasting and prayers (Luke 2:37). Upon seeing baby Jesus, it was revealed to her who He was, and she began to give thanks to God. Just as her name meant "gracious one who gives," Anna also gave the Good News that prophesies were being fulfilled in their presence. The longed-for Redeemer had come!

Come, let us worship and bow down; let us kneel before the Lord our Maker.

Psalm 95:6

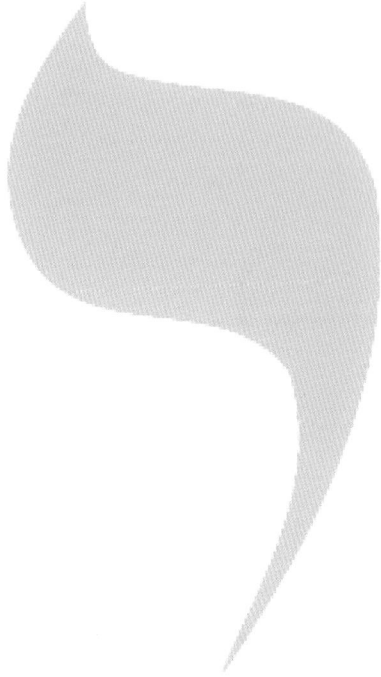

Chapter 10

Wisdom and Adoration

We learn from the Gospel of Matthew that Mary and Joseph did not immediately return to Nazareth after the birth of Jesus. Instead, it is likely that for the first year or more of Jesus' life, He and His parents lived in a house in Bethlehem (Matthew 2:5,11).

It was into this time and place that the next individuals God stirred to seek and worship His son arrived. De-

scribed as "wise men from the east" (Matthew 2:1), these individuals were Magi, men of religious standing. Familiar with at least some Old Testament prophecy regarding the coming of the Messiah, they had witnessed the rising of "His star" and knew the King of the Jews had been born.

Have you ever wondered what Jesus' star looked like? How did the way it appeared reveal such meaning to the Magi? A star of such significance that it prompted them to travel over 1,000 miles to find the One to whom it pointed! Could it be that just as He had done with the shepherds, God brought out "His star" as a supernatural revelation of His Glory? What a wonder it must have been for the Magi to follow it and ultimately discover God's glory in human form—baby Jesus!

It is believed the wise men came from the area of Persia, which is known today as Iran and eastern Iraq. Matthew does not tell us how they traveled, but even with camels or horses, it would have taken them four to five months to arrive in Jerusalem. While they went with the hope of finding the promised Messiah, their limited knowledge of prophecy is evidenced by the fact that they didn't know exactly where to find him. As Jerusalem was the capital of Israel and the seat of governing power, it was logical for them to go there in search of a king. Matthew 1:1 tells us they "arrived in Jerusalem" to inquire about where to find the one "who had been born king of the Jews" so they could worship him.

At that time, Judea was ruled by King Herod. Known historically as Herod the Great, this title only differenti-ated him from other kings of the same name, as his rule

was marked by great paranoia and cruelty. When, amidst political unrest, Rome had declared Herod king of the region over thirty years before, they had given him the title "King of the Jews." Thus, when the wise men arrived asking where they could find the one born king of the Jews, Herod and his court would have been thrown into a panic. Not even fully Jewish by birth or identification, Herod would have been threatened upon hearing of a king *born* into a position into which he had only been placed.

Fueled by insane jealousy and being skilled in trickery, Herod called on the chief priests and scribes to discover that the Christ, or anointed one, was prophesied to be born in Bethlehem. Matthew 1:7-8 tells us he also secretly summoned the wise men to find out the exact time they had seen the star appear. He then sent them to Bethlehem, asking them to report back to him once they found the one of whom was prophesied so that he, too, could go and worship.

Again, we don't know exactly *how* the star led the wise men from Jerusalem to the very place Jesus lived in Bethlehem, but we do know *who* led the star that led the wise men. We read in Isaiah that God, who created the stars, knows how many there are and the name of each. ONLY God could have been responsible for intentionally leading these foreigners to find His Son.

And when they saw him, worship they did! Matthew 2:11 says, "Entering the house, they saw the child with Mary his mother, and falling to their knees, they worshipped him. Then they opened their treasures and presented him with gifts: gold, frankincense, and myrrh."

The story of the wise men ends with their return to their own country *without* returning to Herod. This necessary change of plans was revealed to them as a warning in a dream. Herod's underlying intentions in asking them to return with news of the child were likely unknown to the wise men, but isn't it amazing and wonderful that nothing is hidden from God?

God's redirection of the wise men was immediately followed by another visit from an angel of the Lord; he appeared to Joseph in a dream, saying, "Get up! Take the child and his mother, flee to Egypt, and stay there until I tell you. For Herod is about to search for the child to kill him" (Matthew 2:13). With the same obedience demonstrated throughout our story, Joseph immediately "got up, took the child and his mother during the night, and escaped to Egypt" (Matthew 2:14).

When Herod realized he had been outwitted by the wise men, Matthew 2:16 tells us he flew into a rage. He gave orders to massacre all the boys in and around Bethlehem who were two years old and under, keeping with the time he had learned the star had appeared to the wise men.

It is believed Herod died in 4 B.C. Upon his death, an angel of the Lord again appeared to Joseph in a dream while in Egypt. The angel informed him that it was safe to return to Israel and, in yet another dream, directed him to the region of Galilee.

Thus, Joseph, Mary, and Jesus settled in a town called Nazareth, where Jesus would live until God's purposes for His birth and life would begin to be revealed.

"...choose for your-
selves this day
whom you will
serve.....But as for
me and my house-
hold, we will serve
the Lord."
Joshua 24:15,
NIV

Conclusion

You may have heard that God's plan to send His Son to earth, as part of His great rescue plan for all mankind, was established even before time began (I Corinthians 2:7). In just these few events at which we have looked surrounding Jesus' birth, we have seen God reveal Himself in many miraculous ways when the "right time" came to put His plan in motion. God revealed Himself in wondrous ways by knowing hearts, dispensing angels, guiding through dreams, directing kings, raising stars, and fulfilling numerous prophesies at every turn!

In the introduction, we touched on the fact that the two men, Matthew and Luke, who were led to write about the story of Jesus' birth, geared their Gospel messages to the Jews and Gentiles, respectively. Matthew' declared to the Jews that Jesus IS the Messiah. Luke proclaimed that He is the Messiah—the deliverer—for ALL people!

Throughout the story, we read of many different responses to the revelation of God-made-flesh. Beginning with Zacharias and Elizabeth and continuing with Mary and Joseph, we witnessed faith that believed and humble obedience that followed God despite lack of understanding and hardship. We saw Herod, who was so concerned with his own self-rule and control that he took steps to try to eliminate the very presence of Jesus. And then there were the scribes and Pharisees. They knew the prophecies and would have even testified that they were waiting to see the Messiah. Yet when presented with Him in a manner that did not fit their expectations or lifestyles, they quickly chose to ignore Him. Finally, we learned about the shepherds and wise men who were common laborers and wealthy foreigners who joyfully left their "familiar" to seek and worship the revealed Son of God.

In which of the above individuals do you see yourself? Just as God sent a star to lead the wise men, Jesus is still the bright and morning star for us today (Revelation 22:16). He is worthy of being worshipped in your heart and home this Christmas and all the days of your life.

May the wonder of His power and purposes evidenced in the story of Christ's birth continually command your attention and affection—He deserves it all!

May you, like the wise men, be inspired to rejoice with fresh wonder at God's loving revelation of Himself through His Son, Jesus.

An Invitation

It is our prayer that reading this account of the Christmas story has had a dramatic impact on you. In the Conclusion we asked you to consider the men and women who played a role in God's rescue plan for the world. When faced with the love of God who sent His only Son, Jesus, into the world to be our Savior, we must each decide how we will respond.

Perhaps, like the scribes and Pharisees, you have only wanted Jesus if he fit your terms or conditions. Maybe your desire to remain "in control" and in charge of your own life and destiny, has caused you to completely disregard that he even exists and came to this world to give you His life and a better future.

If reading these pages has made it obvious to you that there is a decision to be made regarding your personal relationship with God, will you choose today to follow the example of those in this story who humbled themselves and chose to believe by faith?

If you said, "Yes", will you now take the following steps? In doing so, we pray you experience firsthand the wonder of God's great and personal love for you!

Admit that you have fallen short of what God intended for you and need a Savior. (I am a sinner)

Confess your failures and sinful thoughts, attitudes, and behaviors, and declare your desire to turn away from such. (Repentance)

Believe that Jesus Christ is the Son of God, who came as a baby, lived as a sinless man, died on the cross for you, and rose from the grave so that you may have eternal life. (Be saved by faith)

Invite Jesus Christ to take charge of your life and show you how to live anew. (Receive Him as Savior and Lord)

Romans 10:9-11b, assures us, "If you confess with your mouth, "Jesus is Lord," and believe in your heart that God raised him from the dead, you will be saved. One believes with the heart, resulting in righteousness, and one confesses with the mouth, resulting in salvation. For Scripture says, Everyone who believes on him will not be put to shame."

If you have responded to God's call on your life and taken these steps, you are now part of God's family! We would also love to hear from you so that we can rejoice with you and encourage you in your faith. You may connect with us at accepted@myQ4impact.org.

Overwhelmed with the Wonder of God,

Ron and Susan

Appendix

Primary Prophecies Fulfilled in Jesus' Birth

Christian Standard Bible (CSB) Translation

Isaiah 40:3 – "A voice of one crying out: Prepare the way of the Lord in the wilderness; make a straight highway for our God in the desert."

Isaiah 7:14 – "Therefore, the Lord himself will give you a sign: See, the virgin will conceive, have a son, and name him Immanuel."

Isaiah 11:1, 2a – "Then a shoot will grow from the stump of Jesse, and a branch from his roots will bear fruit. The Spirit of the Lord will rest on him."

Numbers 24:17 – "I see him but not now; I perceive him, but not near. A star will come from Jacob, and a scepter will arise from Israel."

Jeremiah 23:5-6 – "Look, the days are coming – this is the Lord's declaration – when I will raise up a Righteous Branch for David. He will reign wisely as king and administer justice and righteousness in the land. In his days Judah will be saved, and Israel will dwell securely. This is the name he will be called: The Lord is Our Righteousness."

Micah 5:2 – "Bethlehem Ephrathah, you are small among the clans of Judah; one will come from you to be ruler over Israel for me. His origin is from antiquity, from ancient times."

Psalm 72:9,10 – "May desert tribes kneel before him and his enemies lick the dust. May the kings of Tarshish and the coasts and islands bring tribute, the kings of the Sheba and Seba offer gifts. Let all kings bow in homage to him, all nations serve him."

Jeremiah 31:15 – "This is what the Lord says: A voice was heard in Ramah, a lament with bitter weeping – Rachel weeping for her children, refusing to be comforted for her children because they are no more."

Hosea 11:1 – "When Israel was a child, I loved him, and out of Egypt I called my son."

RON REGENSTREIF loves strategically connecting people and serving those in need around the world. He is passionate about the practical application of Biblical principles in every area and stage of life, and regularly speaks at colleges and conferences on such. Ron has been married to his wife, Roxann, since 1973. They have three sons and are the proud grandparents of five granddaughters and three grandsons. Ron founded Regency Enterprises in 1981 and served as CEO of Regency Lighting for 35+ years. He is currently the Co-Chairman of the Board of Directors for Regency Lighting, and also serves on the Board of Directors for Q4 Impact, Joni & Friends, His Hands on Africa, and Chosen People Ministries.

SUSAN KUNSELMAN has a genuine love for others and for the Word of God. She is passionate about encouraging people in their faith, so they may experience ever-increasing joy and freedom in their lives. Holding degrees in Communication and Pastoral Care and Counseling, Susan has held leadership roles in both business and ministry. Susan was the Corporate Administrator for Regency Lighting for 18 years and is now a writer for Q4 Impact and serves people as a Life Coach. Susan lives in New Hampshire with her much-loved son, Micah.

Recipe for Peanut Butter Cups

NAME OF DISH

FROM THE KITCHEN OF

INGREDIENTS

The Regenstreif Family

One package graham crackers, one box powdered sugar, one cup peanut butter, one cup butter, one 12oz package chocolate chips

DIRECTIONS

Mix: 1 package (out of 3 pkg. box) graham crackers, crumbs, 1 box powdered sugar

Melt: 1 C. peanut butter, 1 C. of butter

Combine all of the above then pack into 9" x 13" pan.

Melt: 1 12-ounce package chocolate chips and spread over the top. Refrigerate. Cut into 1" squares.

Tips: After you follow the first two steps of the recipe, mixing the first four ingredients together with a mixer makes a smoother base. Also, let sit out of the refrigerator for an hour before cutting to keep the chocolate from cracking. These freeze well, so I always make several batches!

To receive two, **FREE** additional recipes that have been favorites at the Regenstreif's annual Christmas Eve celebration, please **Visit Us at www.myQ4impact.org/recipe**

About Q4 Impact

The *Wonder of Christmas* is the opening contribution of Q4 Impact, and we hope it will become part of your most meaningful Christmas celebrations each year.

Q4 Impact was established as a Non-Profit Foundation in early 2022 by a group of individuals who love Jesus and desire to help others identify and learn how to focus well on life's most meaningful priorities.

Q4 Impact seeks to provide inspiration and opportunity, as it encourages others to fully engage their lives in what is truly important. We believe that only through intentional identification of such priorities, will we invest our time, energy, and resources into what will allow us to keep making an impact all the way through the 4th quarter of our lives.

The *Wonder of Christmas* is the first of what we anticipate will be a long line of inspirational and encouraging resources to help you make the most of your life and become who you were created to be.

Please check out our website at www.myQ4impact.org and sign up to be the first to know about upcoming offerings from Q4 Impact.

We hope you enjoyed reading *The Wonder of Christmas.*

If you would like to share additional copies with friends, family, or within your ministry or organization, the book may be purchased at the following locations:

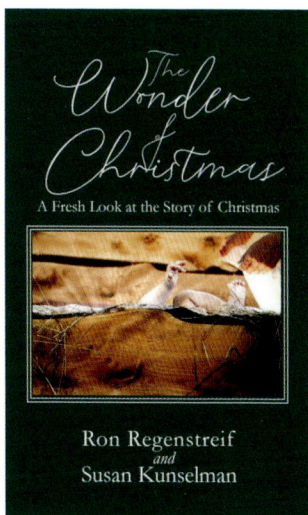

The Wonder of Christmas
A Fresh Look at the Story of Christmas

Ron Regenstreif
and
Susan Kunselman

Click on the QR code to be taken directly to the order form, or use this URL:

http://www.myQ4impact.org/WonderofChristmas

Check out our website for additional, special discounts on larger quantity orders.*

*Discounts on single-book purchases are taken off the Suggested Retail Price of $19.99 and special discount-pricing is available for case-quantity orders (20 books/case).